tapas

_p_

This is a Parragon Book
This edition published in 2005

Parragon
Queen Street House
4 Queen Street
Bath BA1 1HE, UK

ISBN: 1-40543-718-9 (hardback)
ISBN: 1-40543-722-7 (paperback)

Printed in China

Produced by the Bridgewater Book Company Ltd.
Project Designer: Michael Whitehead
Project Editor: Anna Samuels
Photographer: David Jordan
Home Economist: Jacqueline Bellefontaine

Notes for the Reader
This book uses metric and imperial measurements. Follow the
same units of measurement throughout; do not mix metric and
imperial. All spoon measurements are level: teaspoons are
assumed to be 5 ml, and tablespoons are assumed to be 15 ml.
Unless otherwise stated, milk is assumed to be full fat, eggs and
individual vegetables such as potatoes are medium, and pepper
is freshly ground black pepper.

Recipes using raw or very lightly cooked eggs should be avoided by
infants, the elderly, pregnant women, convalescents, and anyone
suffering from an illness. Pregnant and breastfeeding women are
also advised to avoid eating peanuts and peanut products.

contents

introduction

TAPAS dishes are quick and easy to prepare and can be served both hot and cold. Hopping from bar to bar tasting different tapas dishes is part of Spanish life. Tapas are also ideal dishes for serving on special occasions.

Tapas, which originated in Spain, are appetizers that can be served either hot or cold. They are normally served with chilled white wine, beer or sherry and can be found in most bars and wine bars, *tascas* and *bodegas* all over Spain.

They are normally served before lunch and dinner. Tapas are so versatile that they can also be prepared and eaten on special occasions and at parties, either served at the table or presented as part of a buffet selection.

Tapas were invented in Andalusia, a wine-making region in southern Spain. The actual word tapas comes from the Spanish word tapar, which means 'to cover'. Tapa is also the word for 'a lid'. In this region a piece of bread would be placed over a person's wine glass in order to keep the flies and dust away.

The Andalusians then gradually thought of placing other items of food on top of the bread and this is how tapas originated.

It is best to serve the tapas dishes in small earthenware bowls as these are good for keeping the food warm or cold. However, if you do not

have small bowls, ordinary serving dishes will also be fine.

Included in this book is a fine selection of tasty recipes that truly represent traditional food associated with Spain. The number and diversity of tapas that exist are amazing. This book is divided into four parts: Meat & Poultry, Vegetables, Cheese & Eggs, Fish & Seafood.

The Meat & Poultry section includes a wide selection of recipes which draw on chorizo, the popular sausage, chicken, serrano ham and pork.

The Vegetables section is colourful and draws on a range of vegetables such as green beans, aubergines, potatoes, tomatoes and spinach. The Salted Almonds recipe is very popular and really versatile as walnut halves, pistachios, peanuts and cashews can also be used.

The Cheese & Eggs section is equally varied and includes recipes which use Parmesan, Manchego and Cheddar cheese. The Cheese Puffs with Fiery Tomato Salsa is clearly a dish for those who like hot food! If you are able to find Manchego cheese then the Fried Manchego Cheese dish is an excellent tapa to have with chilled wine.

Finally the Fish & Seafood section includes a huge variety of recipes, a reflection of the choice of fish that is on offer in Spain! The Sardines Marinated in Sherry Vinegar are delicious and the same recipe can be made with fresh trout or salmon fillets.

It is a good idea to have cocktail sticks available for the tapas and a small saucer for the discarded sticks.

meat & poultry

INCLUDED in this section are eleven tasty meat and poultry recipes. The chorizo sausage recipes are popular and are very quick and easy to prepare. There are also other equally tasty dishes using chicken, ham and pork.

garlic fried bread
& chorizo

Choose a soft chorizo sausage for this recipe. Although it will not have been cured
for a long period, the soft varieties usually contain a high proportion of fat, which
makes them very good for cooking. As an alternative to chorizo, you could use thickly cut
serrano ham or even garlic sausage. *SERVES 6–8 AS PART OF A TAPAS MEAL*

200 g/7 oz chorizo sausage,
outer casing removed
4 thick slices 2-day-old country bread
Spanish olive oil, for shallow-frying
3 garlic cloves, finely chopped
2 tbsp chopped fresh
flat-leaved parsley
paprika, to garnish

Cut the chorizo sausage into 1-cm/$^1/_2$-inch thick
slices and cut the bread, with its crusts still on,
into 1-cm/$^1/_2$-inch cubes. Add sufficient olive oil
to a large, heavy-based frying pan so that it
generously covers the base. Heat the oil, add the
garlic and fry for 30 seconds–1 minute, or until
lightly browned.

Add the bread cubes to the pan and fry,
stirring all the time, until golden brown and crisp.
Add the chorizo slices and fry for 1–2 minutes, or
until hot. Using a slotted spoon, remove the bread
cubes and chorizo from the pan and drain well on
kitchen paper.

Turn the fried bread and chorizo into a
warmed serving bowl, add the chopped parsley
and toss them together. Garnish the dish with a
sprinkling of paprika and serve warm. Accompany
with cocktail sticks so that a piece of sausage and
a cube of bread can be speared together for eating.

variation

If you are unable to find fresh artichokes, you could use 400 g/14 oz canned artichoke hearts. Drain the juices and slice the artichoke hearts in half. As a variation, you could use serrano ham, cut in one thick piece rather than sliced, instead of the chorizo.

melon, chorizo & artichoke salad

Chorizo is so versatile and can be combined with fruit and vegetables.

SERVES 8 AS PART OF A TAPAS MEAL

12 small globe artichokes

juice of 1/2 lemon

2 tbsp Spanish olive oil

1 small orange-fleshed melon,
such as cantaloupe

200 g/7 oz chorizo sausage,
outer casing removed

few sprigs of fresh tarragon or
flat-leaved parsley, to garnish

dressing

3 tbsp Spanish extra virgin olive oil

1 tbsp red wine vinegar

1 tsp prepared mustard

1 tbsp chopped fresh tarragon

salt and pepper

To prepare the artichokes, cut off the stalks. With your hands, break off the toughest outer leaves at the base until the tender inside leaves are visible. Using a pair of scissors, cut the spiky tips off the leaves. Using a sharp knife, pare the dark green skin from the base and down the stem. As you prepare them, brush the cut surfaces of the artichokes with lemon juice to prevent discoloration. Alternatively, you could fill a bowl with cold water to which you have added a little lemon juice, and immerse the artichokes in the acidulated water to stop discoloration. Carefully remove the choke (the mass of silky hairs) by pulling it out with your fingers or by scooping it out with a spoon. It is very important to remove all the choke, as the little barbs, if eaten, can irritate the throat. However, if you are using very young artichokes, you do not need to worry about removing the choke and you can include the stalk too, well scraped, as it will be quite tender. Cut the artichokes into quarters and brush them again with lemon juice.

Heat the olive oil in a large, heavy-based frying pan, add the prepared artichokes and fry, stirring frequently, for 5 minutes. Remove from the pan, transfer to a large bowl and leave to cool.

To prepare the melon, cut in half and scoop out the seeds with a spoon. Cut the flesh into bite-sized cubes. Add to the cooled artichokes. Cut the chorizo into bite-sized chunks and add to the melon and artichokes.

To make the dressing, put all the ingredients in a small bowl and whisk together. Just before serving, pour the dressing over the prepared salad ingredients and toss together. Serve the salad garnished with tarragon sprigs.

chorizo in red wine

It is also fun to make this dish with small, individual chorizo sausages. Prepare them in exactly the same way but, after removing their outer casing, keep them whole rather than slicing. *SERVES 6 AS PART OF A TAPAS MEAL*

200 g/7 oz chorizo sausage
200 ml/7 fl oz Spanish red wine
2 tbsp brandy (optional)
fresh flat-leaved parsley, to garnish
crusty bread, to serve

Before you begin, bear in mind that this dish is best if prepared the day before you are planning to serve it.

Using a fork, prick the chorizo sausage in 3 or 4 places. Put it in a large saucepan and pour in the wine. Bring the wine to the boil, then reduce the heat, cover and simmer gently for 15–20 minutes. Transfer the chorizo and wine to a bowl or dish, cover, and leave the sausage to marinate in the wine for 8 hours or overnight.

The next day, remove the chorizo from the bowl or dish and reserve the wine for later. Remove the outer casing from the chorizo and cut the sausage into 5-mm/$^1/_4$-inch slices. Place the slices in a large, heavy-based frying pan or flameproof serving dish.

If you are adding the brandy, pour it into a small saucepan and heat gently. Pour the brandy over the chorizo slices, stand well back and set alight. When the flames have died down, shake the pan gently, add the reserved wine to the pan and cook over a high heat until almost all of the wine has evaporated.

Serve the chorizo in red wine piping hot, in the dish in which it was cooked, with parsley to garnish. Accompany with chunks or slices of bread to mop up the juices and provide cocktail sticks to spear the pieces of chorizo.

variation

You can also use cider in place of
the red wine, since it is often used
in the north of Spain.

chorizo empanadillas

A tapas meal would not be complete without the inclusion
of chorizo. In this recipe, it is encased in puff pastry and makes a delicious
accompaniment to a glass of chilled white wine. *MAKES 12*

125 g/4¹/₂ oz chorizo sausage,
outer casing removed
plain flour, for dusting
250 g/9 oz ready-made puff pastry,
thawed if frozen
beaten egg, to glaze
paprika and fresh basil, to garnish

Preheat the oven to 200°C/400°F/Gas Mark 6. Cut the chorizo sausage into small dice measuring about 1 cm/¹/₂ inch square.

On a lightly floured work surface, thinly roll out the puff pastry. Using a plain, round

8-cm/3¹/₄-inch cutter, cut into rounds. Gently pile the trimmings together, roll out again, then cut out further rounds to produce 12 in total. Put about 1 teaspoon of the chopped chorizo onto each of the pastry rounds.

Dampen the edges of the pastry with a little water, then fold one half over the other half to cover the chorizo completely. Seal the edges together with your fingers. Using the prongs of a fork, press against the edges to give a decorative finish and seal them further. With the tip of a sharp knife, make a small slit in the side of each pastry. You can store the pastries in the refrigerator at this stage until you are ready to bake them.

Place the pastries onto dampened baking trays and brush each with a little beaten egg to glaze. Bake in the oven for 10–15 minutes, or until golden brown and puffed. Using a small sieve, lightly dust the top of each empanadilla with a little paprika. Garnish with basil and serve the chorizo empanadillas hot or warm.

cook's tip

The empanadillas are particularly easy to prepare – in fact, something a child might like to make. Just watch that they don't eat all the chorizo before it reaches the oven!

chicken in lemon & garlic

There are several variations to this popular, quick and easy-to-prepare tapa dish.
Try, for example, using chicken wings or, in place of the chicken,
use slices of fresh rabbit, turkey or pork. *SERVES 6–8 AS PART OF A TAPAS MEAL*

4 large skinless, boneless chicken breasts

5 tbsp Spanish olive oil

1 onion, finely chopped

6 garlic cloves, finely chopped

grated rind of 1 lemon, finely pared rind of 1 lemon and juice of both lemons

4 tbsp chopped fresh flat-leaved parsley, plus extra to garnish

salt and pepper

lemon wedges and crusty bread, to serve

Using a sharp knife, slice the chicken breasts widthways into very thin slices. Heat the olive oil in a large, heavy-based frying pan, add the onion and fry for 5 minutes, or until softened but not browned. Add the garlic and fry for a further 30 seconds.

Add the sliced chicken to the pan and fry gently for 5–10 minutes, stirring from time to time, until all the ingredients are lightly browned and the chicken is tender.

Add the grated lemon rind and the lemon juice and let it bubble. At the same time, deglaze the pan by scraping and stirring all the bits on the base of the pan into the juices with a wooden spoon. Remove the pan from the heat, stir in the parsley and season to taste with salt and pepper.

Transfer the chicken in lemon and garlic, piping hot, to a warmed serving dish. Sprinkle with the pared lemon rind, garnish with the parsley and serve with lemon wedges for squeezing over the chicken, accompanied by chunks or slices of crusty bread for mopping up the lemon and garlic juices.

crispy chicken & ham croquettes

These cylindrical croquettes are very popular and served throughout Spain.

MAKES 8

4 tbsp olive oil or 55 g/2 oz butter

4 tbsp plain flour

200 ml/7 fl oz milk

115 g/4 oz cooked chicken, minced

55 g/2 oz serrano or cooked ham, very finely chopped

1 tbsp chopped fresh flat-leaved parsley, plus extra sprigs to garnish

small pinch of freshly grated nutmeg

salt and pepper

1 egg, beaten

55 g/2 oz day-old white breadcrumbs

sunflower oil, for deep-frying

Aïoli (see page 53), to serve

Heat the olive oil in a saucepan. Stir in the flour to form a paste and cook gently, stirring, for 1 minute. Remove the saucepan from the heat and stir in the milk until smooth. Return to the heat and slowly bring to the boil, stirring all the time, until the mixture boils and thickens.

Remove the saucepan from the heat, add the minced chicken and beat until the mixture is smooth. Add the chopped ham, parsley and nutmeg and mix well together. Season the mixture to taste with salt and pepper. Spread the chicken mixture in a dish and leave for 30 minutes, or until cool, then cover and put in the refrigerator for 2–3 hours or overnight. Do not be tempted to miss out this stage, as chilling the croquettes helps to stop them falling apart when they are cooked.

When the chicken mixture has chilled, pour the beaten egg onto a plate and spread the breadcrumbs out on a separate plate. Divide the chicken mixture into 8 equal-sized portions. With dampened hands, form each portion into a cylindrical shape. Dip the croquettes, one at a time, in the beaten egg, then roll in the breadcrumbs to coat them. Place on a plate and chill in the refrigerator for about 1 hour.

To cook the croquettes, heat the oil in a deep fryer to 180–190°C/350–375°F, or until a cube of bread browns in 30 seconds. Add the croquettes, in batches to prevent the temperature of the oil dropping, and fry for 5–10 minutes. Remove from the fryer with a slotted spoon and drain well on kitchen paper.

Serve the chicken and ham croquettes piping hot, garnished with parsley sprigs and accompanied by a bowl of Aïoli for dipping.

cook's tip

These crispy croquettes are another very
popular tapa served all over Spain and come
in an enormous variety of flavours and in all
shapes and sizes, from round and oval to flat
and cylindrical.

variation

You could add some halved or quartered
mushrooms and/or 1 tablespoon of drained
capers or chopped green olives.

chicken livers in sherry sauce

This tapa dish is often served in Andalusia's tapas bars and is equally popular made with lamb's or calf's kidneys.

SERVES 6 AS PART OF A TAPAS MEAL

450 g/1 lb chicken livers
2 tbsp Spanish olive oil
1 small onion, finely chopped
2 garlic cloves, finely chopped

100 ml/3¹/₂ fl oz dry Spanish sherry
salt and pepper
2 tbsp chopped fresh flat-leaved parsley
crusty bread or toast, to serve

If necessary, trim the chicken livers, cutting away any ducts and gristle, then cut them into small, bite-sized pieces.

Heat the olive oil in a large, heavy-based frying pan. Add the onion and fry for 5 minutes, or until softened but not browned. Add the garlic and fry for a further 30 seconds.

Add the chicken livers to the pan and fry for 2–3 minutes, stirring all the time, until they are firm and have changed colour on the outside but are still pink and soft in the centre. Using a slotted spoon, lift the chicken livers from the pan, transfer them to a large, warmed serving dish or several smaller ones and keep warm.

Add the sherry to the pan, increase the heat and let it bubble for 3–4 minutes to evaporate the alcohol and reduce slightly. At the same time, deglaze the pan by scraping and stirring all the bits on the base of the pan into the sauce with a wooden spoon. Season the sauce to taste with salt and pepper.

Pour the sherry sauce over the chicken livers and sprinkle over the parsley. Serve piping hot, accompanied by chunks or slices of crusty bread or toast to mop up the sherry sauce.

broad beans with serrano ham

Both fresh and dried broad beans are highly regarded in Spain.
In this recipe, you can use fresh or, if more convenient, frozen broad beans,
but if you choose the latter, make sure that they are baby ones, which
are more tender. If you have time, you can remove the skins from the beans to reveal
the soft, bright-green bean inside, but it is a time-consuming task!

SERVES 6–8 AS PART OF A TAPAS MEAL

55 g/2 oz serrano or Parma ham, pancetta
or rindless smoked streaky bacon
115 g/4 oz chorizo sausage,
outer casing removed
4 tbsp Spanish olive oil
1 onion, finely chopped
2 garlic cloves, finely chopped
splash of dry white wine
450 g/1 lb frozen broad beans, thawed,
or about 1.3 kg/3 lb fresh broad beans in
their pods, shelled to give 450 g/1 lb
1 tbsp chopped fresh dill or mint,
plus extra to garnish
pinch of sugar
salt and pepper

Using a sharp knife, cut the ham, pancetta or bacon into small strips. Cut the chorizo into 2-cm/3/4-inch cubes. Heat the olive oil in a large, heavy-based frying pan or flameproof dish that has a lid. Add the onion and fry for 5 minutes, or until softened and beginning to brown. If you are using pancetta or bacon, add it with the onion. Add the garlic and fry for a further 30 seconds.

Pour the wine into the pan, increase the heat and let it bubble to evaporate the alcohol, then reduce the heat. Add the broad beans, ham, if using, and the chorizo and fry for 1–2 minutes, stirring all the time to coat in the oil.

Cover the pan and let the beans simmer very gently in the oil, stirring from time to time, for 10–15 minutes, or until the beans are tender. It may be necessary to add a little water to the pan during cooking, so keep an eye on it and add a splash if the beans appear to become too dry. Stir in the dill and sugar. Season the dish with salt and pepper, but taste first because you may find that it does not need any salt.

Transfer the broad beans to a large, warmed serving dish, several smaller ones or individual plates, and serve piping hot, garnished with chopped dill.

tiny spanish meat balls
in almond sauce

Minced pork, or a combination of pork and veal, is the most traditional meat used in Spain to make these meatballs, but there is no reason why you could not use lamb or beef mince, if preferred.

SERVES 6–8 AS PART OF A TAPAS MEAL

55 g/2 oz white or brown bread,
crusts removed

3 tbsp water

450 g/1 lb fresh lean pork mince

1 large onion, finely chopped

1 garlic clove, crushed

2 tbsp chopped fresh
flat-leaved parsley, plus extra to garnish

1 egg, beaten

freshly grated nutmeg

salt and pepper

flour, for coating

2 tbsp Spanish olive oil

squeeze of lemon juice

crusty bread, to serve

Almond Sauce

2 tbsp Spanish olive oil

25 g/1 oz white or brown bread

115 g/4 oz blanched almonds

2 garlic cloves, finely chopped

150 ml/5 fl oz dry white wine

salt and pepper

425 ml/15 fl oz vegetable stock

To prepare the meatballs, put the bread in a bowl, add the water and leave to soak for 5 minutes. With your hands, squeeze out the water and return the bread to the dried bowl. Add the pork, onion, garlic, parsley and egg, then season generously with grated nutmeg and a little salt and pepper. Knead the ingredients well together to form a smooth mixture.

Spread some flour on a plate. With floured hands, shape the meat mixture into about 30 equal-sized balls, then roll each meatball again in flour until coated.

Heat the olive oil in a large, heavy-based frying pan, add the meatballs, in batches so that they do not overcrowd the pan, and fry for 4–5 minutes, or until browned on all sides. Using a slotted spoon, remove the meatballs from the pan and set aside.

To make the almond sauce, heat the olive oil in the same frying pan in which the meatballs were fried. Break the bread into pieces, add to the pan with the almonds and fry gently, stirring frequently, until the bread and almonds are golden brown. Add the garlic and fry for a further

30 seconds, then pour in the wine and boil for 1–2 minutes. Season to taste with salt and pepper and allow to cool slightly.

Transfer the almond mixture to a food processor. Pour in the vegetable stock and blend the mixture until smooth. Return the sauce to the frying pan.

Carefully add the fried meatballs to the almond sauce and simmer for 25 minutes, or until the meatballs are tender. Taste the sauce and season with salt and pepper if necessary.

Transfer the cooked meatballs and almond sauce to a warmed serving dish, then add a squeeze of lemon juice to taste and sprinkle with chopped parsley to garnish.

This dish is best served piping hot with chunks or slices of crusty bread for mopping up the almond sauce.

roasted asparagus
with mountain ham

The most popular Spanish ham is serrano, which means mountain ham, because it is cured in the mountains. It is then aged from several months to several years. If you are unable to obtain it, you could use Italian Parma ham or prosciutto instead. *MAKES 12*

2 tbsp Spanish olive oil

6 slices serrano ham

12 asparagus spears

pepper

Aïoli (see page 53), to serve

Preheat the oven to 200°C/400°F/Gas Mark 6. Put half the olive oil in a roasting tin that will hold the asparagus spears in a single layer and swirl it around so that it covers the base. Cut each slice of serrano ham in half lengthways.

Trim the ends of the asparagus spears, then wrap a slice of ham around the stem end of each spear. Place the wrapped spears in the prepared roasting tin and lightly brush the ham and asparagus with the remaining olive oil. Season the spears with pepper.

Roast the asparagus spears in the oven for about 10 minutes, depending on the thickness of the asparagus, until tender but still firm. Do not overcook the asparagus spears because it is important that they are still firm, so that you can pick them up with your fingers.

Serve the roasted asparagus with mountain ham piping hot, with a bowl of Aïoli for dipping.

miniature pork brochettes

Although usually made with pork in Spain, these brochettes are of Arab origin
and would be made using lamb; both are delicious. *MAKES 12*

450 g/1 lb lean boneless pork

3 tbsp Spanish olive oil, plus extra
for oiling (optional)

grated rind and juice of
1 large lemon

2 garlic cloves, crushed

2 tbsp chopped fresh flat-leaved parsley,
plus extra to garnish

1 tbsp ras-el-hanout spice blend

salt and pepper

The brochettes are marinated overnight, so remember to do this in advance, in order that they are ready when you need them. Cut the pork into pieces about 2 cm/3/4 inch square and put in a large, shallow, non-metallic dish that will hold the pieces in a single layer.

To prepare the marinade, put all the remaining ingredients in a bowl and mix well together. Pour the marinade over the pork and toss the meat in it until well coated. Cover the dish and

leave to marinate in the refrigerator for 8 hours or overnight, stirring the pork 2–3 times.

You can use wooden or metal skewers to cook the brochettes, and for this recipe you will need about 12 x 15-cm/6-inch skewers. If you are using wooden ones, soak them in cold water for about 30 minutes prior to using. This helps to stop them burning and the food sticking to them during cooking. Metal skewers simply need to be greased, and flat ones should be used in preference to round ones to prevent the food on them falling off.

Preheat the grill, griddle or barbecue. Thread about 3 marinated pork pieces, leaving a little space between each piece, onto each prepared skewer. Cook the brochettes for 10–15 minutes, or until tender and lightly charred, turning several times and basting with the remaining marinade during cooking. Serve the pork brochettes piping hot, garnished with parsley.

cook's tip

The ras-el-hanout spice blend consists of
galangal, rosebuds, black peppercorns,
ginger, cardamon, nigella, cayenne, allspice,
lavender, cinnamon, cassia, coriander, mace,
nutmeg and cloves!

vegetables

THE tapas dishes presented here are delicious and very colourful. From Stuffed Cherry Tomatoes and Roasted Pepper Salad to Spanish Spinach & Tomato Pizzas, every recipe offers a selection of mouthwatering morsels.

cracked marinated olives

The olives will keep in the refrigerator for several months. In fact, the longer
you marinate them, the more their flavour will be enhanced. Use the oil in which
they have been marinated for cooking or in a salad dressing.
It will impart a delicious flavour to a dish. *SERVES 8 AS PART OF A TAPAS MEAL*

450 g/1 lb can or jar unstoned large green
olives, drained

4 garlic cloves, peeled

2 tsp coriander seeds

1 small lemon

4 sprigs of fresh thyme

4 feathery stalks of fennel

2 small fresh red chillies (optional)

pepper

Spanish extra virgin olive oil, to cover

To allow the flavours of the marinade to penetrate the olives, place on a chopping board and, using a rolling pin, bash them lightly so that they crack slightly. Alternatively, use a sharp knife to cut a lengthways slit in each olive as far as the stone. Using the flat side of a broad knife, lightly crush each garlic clove. Using a pestle and mortar, crack the coriander seeds. Cut the lemon, with its rind, into small chunks.

Put the olives, garlic, coriander seeds, lemon chunks, thyme sprigs, fennel and chillies, if using, in a large bowl and toss together. Season with pepper to taste, but you should not need to add salt since conserved olives are usually salty enough. Pack the ingredients tightly into a glass jar with a lid. Pour in enough olive oil to cover the olives, then seal the jar tightly.

Leave the olives at room temperature for 24 hours, then marinate in the refrigerator for at least 1 week, preferably 2 weeks. From time to time, gently give the jar a shake to re-mix the ingredients. Return the olives to room temperature and remove from the oil to serve. Provide cocktail sticks for spearing the olives.

salted almonds

Almonds are the most popular nut to be salted and served as a tapa in Spain, but hazelnuts are also popular and can be prepared in exactly the same way. Walnut halves, pistachios, peanuts and cashews could also be given the same treatment. *SERVES 6–8 AS PART OF A TAPAS MEAL*

225 g/8 oz whole almonds, in their skins or blanched (see method)

4 tbsp Spanish olive oil

coarse sea salt

1 tsp paprika or ground cumin (optional)

Preheat the oven to 180°C/350°F/Gas Mark 4. Fresh almonds in their skins are superior in taste, but blanched almonds are much more convenient. If the almonds are not blanched, put them in a bowl, cover with boiling water for 3–4 minutes, then plunge them into cold water for 1 minute. Drain them well in a sieve, then slide off the skins between your fingers. Dry the almonds well on kitchen paper.

Put the olive oil in a roasting tin and swirl it around so that it covers the base. Add the almonds and toss them in the tin so that they are evenly coated in the oil, then spread them out in a single layer.

Roast the whole almonds in the oven for 20 minutes, or until they are light golden brown,

tossing several times during the cooking. Drain the almonds on kitchen paper, then transfer them to a bowl.

While the almonds are still warm, sprinkle with plenty of sea salt and the paprika, if using, and toss well together to coat. Serve the almonds warm or cold. The almonds are at their best when served freshly cooked, so, if possible, cook them on the day that you plan to eat them. However, they can be stored in an airtight tin for up to 3 days.

sautéed garlic mushrooms

Wild mushrooms such as boletuses or chanterelles can be used in place of cultivated mushrooms. *SERVES 6 AS PART OF A TAPAS MEAL*

450 g/1 lb button mushrooms

5 tbsp Spanish olive oil

2 garlic cloves, finely chopped

squeeze of lemon juice

salt and pepper

4 tbsp chopped fresh

flat-leaved parsley

crusty bread, to serve

Wipe or brush clean the mushrooms, then trim off the stalks close to the caps. Cut the large mushrooms in half or into quarters. Heat the olive oil in a large, heavy-based frying pan, add the garlic and fry for 30 seconds–1 minute, or until lightly browned.

Add the mushrooms and sauté over a high heat, stirring most of the time, until they have absorbed all of the oil in the frying pan.

Reduce the heat to low. When the juices have come out of the mushrooms, increase the heat again and sauté for 4–5 minutes, stirring most of the time, until the juices have almost evaporated. Add a squeeze of lemon juice and season to taste with salt and pepper. Stir in the parsley and cook for a further 1 minute.

Transfer the sautéed mushrooms to a warmed serving dish and serve piping hot or warm. Accompany with chunks or slices of crusty bread for mopping up the garlic cooking juices.

variation

Courgettes may also be prepared in the same way, with a finely chopped small onion fried in the oil until lightly browned before adding the garlic.

stuffed cherry tomatoes

Cherry tomatoes are made for just one mouthful but, if you prefer,
larger tomatoes could be stuffed with the fillings.
The quantities given in the recipe will fill about 10 medium tomatoes.

SERVES 8 AS PART OF A TAPAS MEAL

24 cherry tomatoes

Anchovy & Olive Filling
50 g/1³/4 oz canned anchovy fillets in olive oil
8 pimiento-stuffed green olives, finely chopped
2 large hard-boiled eggs, finely chopped
pepper

OR
Crab Mayonnaise Filling
175 g/6 oz canned crabmeat, drained
4 tbsp mayonnaise
1 tbsp chopped fresh
flat-leaved parsley
salt and pepper

OR
Black Olive & Caper Filling
12 stoned black olives
3 tbsp capers
6 tbsp Aïoli (see page 53)
salt and pepper

Several different choices of filling have been given in this recipe, so make a decision before you begin. Alternatively, of course, you could make a selection of each. Simply cut the filling quantities to stuff the corresponding number of tomatoes.

If necessary, cut and discard a very thin slice from the stalk end of each tomato to make the bases flat and stable. Cut a thin slice from the smooth end of each tomato and reserve for lids. Using a serrated knife or teaspoon, loosen the pulp and seeds of each and scoop out, discarding the flesh. Turn the scooped-out tomatoes upside down on kitchen paper and leave to drain for 5 minutes.

To make the anchovy and olive filling, drain the anchovies, reserving the oil for later, chop finely and put in a bowl. Add the olives and hard-boiled eggs. Pour in a trickle of oil from the drained anchovies to moisten the mixture, season with pepper (do not add salt to season, as the anchovies are salted) and mix well together.

To make the crab mayonnaise filling, put the crabmeat, mayonnaise and parsley in a bowl and mix well together. Season the filling to taste.

To make the black olive and caper filling, put the olives and capers on kitchen paper to drain them well, then chop finely and put in a bowl. Add the Aïoli and mix well together. Season the filling to taste with salt and pepper.

Fill a piping bag fitted with a 2-cm/3/4-inch plain nozzle with the filling of your choice and use to pack the filling into the hollow tomato shells. Store the tomatoes in the refrigerator until ready to serve.

cook's tip
This dip is also very good served
with cold meats.

aubergine & pepper dip

Instead of cooking the aubergines and peppers in the oven,
they can be cooked under the grill until the skins are charred all over.
They do, however, need to be turned frequently and they will
take about 10 minutes. *SERVES 6–8 AS PART OF A TAPAS MEAL*

Preheat the oven to 190°C/375°F/Gas Mark 5. Prick the skins of the aubergines and peppers all over with a fork and brush with about 1 tablespoon of the olive oil. Put on a baking tray and bake in the oven for 45 minutes, or until the skins are beginning to turn black, the flesh of the aubergine is very soft and the peppers are deflated.

When the vegetables are cooked, put them in a bowl and immediately cover tightly with a clean, damp tea towel. Alternatively, you can put the vegetables in a polythene bag. Leave them for about 15 minutes, or until they are cool enough to handle.

When the vegetables have cooled, cut the aubergines in half lengthways, carefully scoop out the flesh and discard the skin. Cut the aubergine flesh into large chunks. Remove and discard the stem, core and seeds from the peppers and cut the flesh into large pieces.

Heat the remaining olive oil in a large, heavy-based frying pan, add the aubergine flesh and pepper pieces and fry for 5 minutes. Add the garlic and fry for a further 30 seconds.

2 large aubergines

2 red peppers

4 tbsp Spanish olive oil

2 garlic cloves, roughly chopped

grated rind and juice of 1/2 lemon

1 tbsp chopped fresh coriander,
    plus extra sprigs to garnish

1/2–1 tsp paprika

salt and pepper

bread or toast, to serve

Turn all the contents of the frying pan onto kitchen paper to drain, then transfer to the bowl of a food processor. Add the lemon rind and juice, the chopped coriander, the paprika, and salt and pepper according to taste, and blend until a speckled purée is formed.

Turn the aubergine and pepper dip into a serving bowl. Serve warm, at room temperature, or leave to cool for 30 minutes, then chill in the refrigerator for at least 1 hour and serve cold. Garnish with coriander sprigs and accompany with thick slices of bread or toast for dipping.

stuffed pimientos

Make sure that you buy whole peppers, not sliced. *MAKES 7–8*

There is actually a choice of fillings provided in this recipe – the final decision is yours. Lift the peppers from the jar, reserving the oil for later.

To make the curd cheese and herb filling, put the curd cheese in a bowl and add the lemon juice, garlic, parsley, mint and oregano. Mix well together. Season to taste with salt and pepper.

To make the tuna mayonnaise filling, put the tuna in a bowl and add the mayonnaise, lemon juice and parsley. Add 1 tablespoon of the reserved oil from the jar of pimientos and mix well. Season to taste with salt and pepper.

To make the goat's cheese and olive filling, put the olives in a bowl and add the goat's cheese, garlic and 1 tablespoon of the reserved oil from the jar of pimientos. Mix well together. Season to taste with salt and pepper.

Using a teaspoon, heap the filling of your choice into each pimiento. Put in the refrigerator and chill for at least 2 hours until firm.

To serve the pimientos, arrange them on a serving plate and, if necessary, wipe with kitchen paper to remove any of the filling that has spread over the skins. Garnish with herb sprigs.

185 g/6¹/₂ oz canned or bottled whole
    pimientos del piquillo
    (chargrilled sweet red peppers)
salt and pepper
fresh herb sprigs, to garnish

Curd Cheese & Herb Filling
225 g/8 oz curd cheese
1 tsp lemon juice
1 garlic clove, crushed
4 tbsp chopped fresh flat-leaved parsley
1 tbsp chopped fresh mint
1 tbsp chopped fresh oregano
salt and pepper

OR
Tuna Mayonnaise Filling
200 g/7 oz canned tuna steak
    in olive oil, drained
5 tbsp mayonnaise
2 tsp lemon juice
2 tbsp chopped fresh flat-leaved parsley
salt and pepper

OR

Goat's Cheese & Olive Filling

50 g/1³/₄ oz stoned black olives,
    finely chopped

200 g/7 oz soft goat's cheese

1 garlic clove, crushed

salt and pepper

variation

Pimiento is simply the Spanish word for
pepper, but outside Spain the word is used to
refer to red peppers that are cooked, peeled
and sold in jars or cans. If you cannot find
pimientos del piquillo, look for a jar of
peppadew peppers from South Africa. This
recipe will fill about 36 peppadew peppers.

variation

Red and yellow peppers have been used here,
but there's no reason why you cannot use
green ones or a mixture.

roasted pepper salad

Although called roasted peppers, the peppers for this recipe are more usually grilled than roasted in an oven. You can also spear them on a fork and hold them over a gas flame, or roast them on a barbecue.

SERVES 8 AS PART OF A TAPAS MEAL

3 red peppers

3 yellow peppers

5 tbsp Spanish extra virgin olive oil

2 tbsp dry sherry vinegar or lemon juice

2 garlic cloves, crushed

pinch of sugar

salt and pepper

1 tbsp capers

8 small black Spanish olives

2 tbsp chopped fresh marjoram, plus extra sprigs to garnish

Preheat the grill. Place all the peppers on a wire rack or grill pan and cook under a hot grill for 10 minutes, or until their skins have blackened and blistered all over, turning them frequently.

Remove the roasted peppers from the heat, put them in a bowl and immediately cover tightly with a clean, damp tea towel.

Alternatively, you can put the peppers in a polythene bag. You will find that the steam helps to soften the skins and makes it easier to remove them. Leave the peppers for about 15 minutes, or until they are cool enough to handle.

Holding one pepper at a time over a clean bowl, use a sharp knife to make a small hole in the base and gently squeeze out the juices and reserve them. Still holding the pepper over the bowl, carefully peel off the blackened skin with your fingers or a knife and discard it. Cut the peppers in half and remove the stem, core and seeds, then cut each pepper into neat thin strips. Arrange the pepper strips attractively on a serving dish.

To the reserved pepper juices add the olive oil, sherry vinegar, garlic, sugar and salt and pepper to taste. Whisk together until combined. Drizzle the dressing evenly over the salad.

Scatter the capers, olives and chopped marjoram over the salad, garnish with marjoram sprigs and serve at room temperature.

variation

This is one of Spain's most popular and staple tapas bar dishes. It varies, but the basic salad consists of potatoes, carrots and peas, and sometimes tuna, as in this recipe.

russian salad

A very popular and colourful dish that can be stored in the fridge.

SERVES 8 AS PART OF A TAPAS MEAL

2 eggs

450 g/1 lb baby new potatoes, quartered

115 g/4 oz fine green beans, cut into
2.5-cm/1-inch lengths

115 g/4 oz frozen peas

115 g/4 oz carrots

200 g/7 oz canned tuna steak in olive oil, drained

2 tbsp lemon juice

8 tbsp mayonnaise

1 garlic clove, crushed

salt and pepper

4 small gherkins, sliced

8 stoned black olives, halved

1 tbsp capers

1 tbsp chopped fresh
flat-leaved parsley

1 tbsp chopped fresh dill, plus
extra sprigs to garnish

Put the eggs in a saucepan, cover with cold water and slowly bring to the boil. Immediately reduce the heat to very low, cover and simmer gently for 10 minutes. As soon as the eggs are cooked, drain them and put under cold running water until they are cold. By doing this quickly, you will prevent a black ring from forming around the egg yolk. Gently tap the eggs to crack the eggshells and leave them until cold.

Meanwhile, put the potatoes in a large saucepan of cold, salted water and bring to the boil. Reduce the heat and simmer for 7 minutes, or until tender. Add the beans and peas to the saucepan for the last 2 minutes of cooking. Drain well, splash under cold running water, then leave the vegetables to cool completely.

Cut the carrots into julienne strips about 2.5 cm/1 inch in length. Flake the tuna into large chunks. When the potatoes, beans and peas are cold, put them in a large bowl. Add the carrot and the tuna and toss the ingredients together. Transfer the vegetables and tuna to a large dish.

In a jug, stir the lemon juice into the mayonnaise to thin it slightly, stir in the garlic and season to taste with salt and pepper. Drizzle the mayonnaise dressing over the vegetables and tuna.

Scatter the gherkins, olives and capers into the salad, sprinkle over the parsley and dill. Store the salad in the refrigerator but return to room temperature before serving. Peel the eggs and slice into wedges, add them to the salad and garnish with dill sprigs.

fried potatoes
with piquant paprika

A variation is to fry the potatoes as here, then spoon over the Fiery Tomato Salsa that accompanies the Cheese Puffs (see page 62) or serve the salsa separately for dipping the potatoes in. This dish is then known as Patatas Bravas (Bold Potatoes). *SERVES 6 AS PART OF A TAPAS MEAL*

3 tsp paprika

1 tsp ground cumin

$^1/_4$–$^1/_2$ tsp cayenne pepper

$^1/_2$ tsp salt

450 g/1 lb small old potatoes, peeled

sunflower oil, for shallow-frying

Aïoli (see page 53), to serve (optional)

Put the paprika, cumin, the cayenne pepper and salt in a small bowl and mix well together. Set aside.

Cut each potato into 8 thick wedges. Pour enough sunflower oil into a large, heavy-based frying pan so that it comes about 2.5 cm/1 inch up the sides of the pan. Heat the oil, then add the potato wedges, preferably in a single layer, and fry gently for 10 minutes turning from time to time.

Remove from the pan with a slotted spoon and drain on kitchen paper. Transfer the potato wedges to a large bowl and, while still hot, sprinkle them with the paprika mixture, then gently toss them together to coat.

Turn the fried potatoes with paprika into one large, warmed serving dish, several smaller ones or individual plates and serve hot. Accompany with a bowl of Aïoli for dipping, if wished.

baby potatoes with Aïoli

The recipe given here for Aïoli contains raw egg and therefore
should be avoided by infants, the elderly, pregnant women, convalescents,
and anyone suffering from an illness. If any of these cases applies to you,
use commercially made mayonnaise and add the crushed garlic to it.

SERVES 6–8 AS PART OF A TAPAS MEAL

450 g/1 lb baby new potatoes

1 tbsp chopped fresh
flat-leaved parsley

salt

Aïoli

1 large egg yolk, at room temperature

1 tbsp white wine vinegar or lemon juice

2 large garlic cloves, peeled

salt and pepper

5 tbsp Spanish extra virgin olive oil

5 tbsp sunflower oil

To make the Aïoli, put the egg yolk, vinegar, garlic and salt and pepper to taste in a bowl and whisk until all ingredients blend well together. Add the olive, then the sunflower oil, drop by drop at first, and then, when it begins to thicken, in a slow, steady stream until the sauce is thick and smooth.

For this recipe, the Aïoli should be a little thin so that it coats the potatoes. To ensure this, quickly blend in 1 tablespoon water so that it forms the consistency of sauce.

To prepare the potatoes, cut them in half or quarters to make bite-sized pieces. If they are very small, you can leave them whole. Put the potatoes in a large saucepan of cold, salted water and bring to the boil. Reduce the heat and simmer for 7 minutes, or until just tender. Drain well, then turn out into a large bowl.

While the potatoes are still warm, gently dip them in the Aïoli sauce. Dipping the potatoes in the sauce will help them to absorb the garlic flavour. Leave the potatoes for about 20 minutes to marinate in the sauce.

Transfer the potatoes with Aïoli to a warmed serving dish, sprinkle over the parsley and salt to taste and serve warm. Alternatively, the dish can be prepared ahead and stored in the refrigerator, but return it to room temperature before serving.

spanish spinach
& tomato pizzas

One associates pizzas with Italy, but these Spanish pizzas are, in fact, very popular tapas dishes.
They were traditionally made from a simple dough of flour and water, but now a bread
or pastry base is used. The toppings can vary too and might include anchovies,
peppers, ham, chorizo sausage and olives, but seldom cheese. *MAKES 32*

**2 tbsp Spanish olive oil, plus extra for
brushing and drizzling
1 onion, finely chopped
1 garlic clove, finely chopped
400 g/14 oz canned chopped tomatoes
125 g/4¹/2 oz baby spinach leaves
salt and pepper
25 g/1 oz pine kernels**

Bread Dough
**4 tbsp warm water
¹/2 tsp easy-blend dried yeast
pinch of sugar
200 g/7 oz strong white flour, plus
extra for dusting
¹/2 tsp salt**

To make the bread dough, measure the water into a small bowl, sprinkle in the dried yeast and sugar and leave in a warm place for 10–15 minutes, or until frothy.

Meanwhile, sift the flour and salt into a large bowl. Make a well in the centre of the flour and pour in the yeast liquid, then mix together with a wooden spoon. Using your hands, work the mixture until it leaves the sides of the bowl clean.

Turn the dough out onto a lightly floured work surface and knead for 10 minutes, or until smooth and elastic and no longer sticky. Shape into a ball and put it in a clean bowl. Cover with a clean, damp tea towel and leave in a warm place for 1 hour, or until it has risen and doubled in size.

To make the topping, heat the olive oil in a large, heavy-based frying pan. Add the onion and fry for 5 minutes, or until softened but not browned. Add the garlic and fry for a further 30 seconds. Stir in the tomatoes and cook for 5 minutes, letting it bubble and stirring occasionally, until reduced to a thick mixture. Add the spinach leaves and cook, stirring, until they

have wilted a little. Season the mixture to taste with salt and pepper.

While the dough is rising, preheat the oven to 200°C/400°F/Gas Mark 6. Brush several baking trays with olive oil. Turn the dough out onto a lightly floured work surface and knead well for 2–3 minutes to knock out the air bubbles. Roll out the dough very, very thinly and, using a 6-cm/2¹/₂-inch plain, round cutter, cut out 32 rounds. Place on the prepared baking sheets.

Spread each base with the spinach mixture to cover, then sprinkle the pine kernels over the top. Drizzle a little olive oil over each pizza. Bake in the oven for 10–15 minutes, or until the edges of the dough are golden brown. Serve the spinach and tomato pizzas hot.

courgette fritters
with a dipping sauce

The exact same treatment can be applied to aubergines, while
the Pine Kernel Sauce can be made with almonds in exactly the same
way too, if preferred. *SERVES 8 AS PART OF A TAPAS MEAL*

Whichever sauce you have chosen, make this first. To make the pine kernel sauce, put the pine kernels and the garlic in a food processor and blend to form a purée. With the motor still running, gradually add the olive oil, lemon juice and water to form a smooth sauce. Stir in the parsley and season to taste with salt and pepper. Turn into a serving bowl.

To prepare the courgettes, cut them on the diagonal into thin slices about 5 mm/1/4 inch thick. Put the flour and paprika in a polythene bag and mix together. Beat the egg and milk together in a large bowl.

Add the courgette slices to the flour mixture and toss well together until coated. Shake off the excess flour. Heat the sunflower oil in a large, heavy-based frying pan to a depth of about 1 cm/1/2 inch. Dip the courgette slices, one at a time, into the egg mixture, then slip them into the hot oil. Fry the courgette slices, in batches of a single layer for 2 minutes, or until crisp and golden brown.

Using a slotted spoon, remove the courgette fritters from the pan and drain on kitchen paper.

450 g/1 lb baby courgettes

3 tbsp plain flour

1 tsp paprika

1 large egg

2 tbsp milk

sunflower oil, for shallow-frying

coarse sea salt

dipping sauce such as Aïoli (see page 53),
    Fiery Tomato Salsa (see page 62)
        or Pine Kernel Sauce (see below)

Pine Kernel Sauce

100 g/3 1/2 oz pine kernels

1 garlic clove, peeled

3 tbsp Spanish extra virgin olive oil

1 tbsp lemon juice

3 tbsp water

1 tbsp chopped fresh flat-leaved parsley

salt and pepper

Continue until all the slices have been fried. Serve the courgette fritters piping hot, lightly sprinkled with sea salt. Accompany with a bowl of your chosen dipping sauce.

green beans
with pine kernels

As a variation to the pine kernels, you could use flaked or blanched almonds, which should be sliced into thin strips before frying. They are equally delicious – it is simply a matter of personal preference. *SERVES 8 AS PART OF A TAPAS MEAL*

2 tbsp Spanish olive oil

50 g/1³/4 oz pine kernels

¹/₂–1 tsp paprika

450 g/1 lb green beans

1 small onion, finely chopped

1 garlic clove, finely chopped

salt and pepper

juice of ¹/₂ lemon

Heat the oil in a large, heavy-based frying pan, add the pine kernels and fry for about 1 minute, stirring all the time and shaking the pan, until light golden brown. Using a slotted spoon, remove the pine kernels from the pan, drain well on kitchen paper, then transfer to a bowl. Reserve the oil in the frying pan for later. Add the paprika, according to taste, to the pine kernels, stir together until coated, and then set aside.

If desired, top and tail the green beans and remove any strings if necessary. Put the beans in a saucepan, pour over boiling water, return to the boil and cook for 5 minutes, or until tender but still firm. Drain well in a colander.

Reheat the oil in the frying pan, add the onion and fry for 5–10 minutes, or until softened and beginning to brown. Add the garlic and fry for a further 30 seconds.

Add the beans to the pan and cook for 2–3 minutes, tossing together with the onion until heated through. Season the beans to taste with salt and pepper.

Turn the contents of the pan into a warmed serving dish, sprinkle over the lemon juice and toss together. Scatter over the golden pine kernels and serve hot.

cheese & eggs

CHEESE and eggs are the basis of a wide range of tapas dishes. There are five recipes in this section, including the well-known Tortilla Española and dishes using a variety of cheeses such as Manchego, Parmesan and Cheddar.

cheese puffs
with fiery tomato salsa

These crisp little cheese puffs are light and fluffy. In this recipe they are served with a salsa, but they can, if preferred, simply be accompanied by small pickled cucumbers. Serve these speared on cocktail sticks so that a pickled cucumber and a cheese puff can be eaten together.

SERVES 8 AS PART OF A TAPAS MEAL

70 g/2¹/₂ oz plain flour

50 ml/2 fl oz Spanish olive oil

150 ml/5 fl oz water

2 eggs, beaten

55 g/2 oz Manchego, Parmesan, Cheddar,
Gouda or Gruyère cheese, finely grated

¹/₂ tsp paprika

salt and pepper

sunflower oil, for deep-frying

Fiery Tomato Salsa

2 tbsp Spanish olive oil

1 small onion, finely chopped

1 garlic clove, crushed

splash of dry white wine

400 g/14 oz canned chopped tomatoes

1 tbsp tomato purée

¹/₄–¹/₂ tsp red chilli pepper flakes

dash of Tabasco sauce

pinch of sugar

salt and pepper

To make the salsa, heat the olive oil in a saucepan, add the onion and fry for 5 minutes, or until softened but not browned. Add the garlic and fry for a further 30 seconds. Add the wine and allow to bubble, then add all the remaining salsa ingredients to the saucepan and simmer, uncovered, for 10–15 minutes, or until a thick sauce is formed. Spoon into a serving bowl and set aside until ready to serve.

Meanwhile, prepare the cheese puffs. Sift the flour onto a plate or sheet of greaseproof paper. Put the olive oil and water in a saucepan and slowly bring to the boil. As soon as the water boils, remove the saucepan from the heat and quickly tip in the flour all at once. Using a wooden spoon, beat the mixture well until it is smooth and leaves the sides of the saucepan.

Leave the mixture to cool for 1–2 minutes, add the eggs, beating hard after each addition and keeping the mixture stiff. Add the cheese and paprika, season to taste with salt and pepper and mix well. Store the mixture in the refrigerator until you are ready to fry the cheese puffs.

Just before serving the cheese puffs, heat the sunflower oil in a deep fryer to 180–190°C/350–375°F, or until a cube of bread browns in 30 seconds. Drop teaspoonfuls of the prepared mixture, in batches, into the hot oil and fry for 2–3 minutes, turning once, or until golden brown and crispy. They should rise to the surface of the oil and puff up. Drain well on kitchen paper.

Serve the puffs piping hot, accompanied by the fiery salsa for dipping and cocktail sticks to spear the puffs.

cheese & olive empanadillas

Since there are not many Spanish cheeses available outside Spain, you can choose to make these pastries with Manchego, Cheddar, Gruyère, Gouda, mozzarella or a firm goat's cheese. Large versions of these empanadillas are known as empanadas. *MAKES 26*

85 g/3 oz firm or soft cheese

85 g/3 oz stoned green olives

55 g/2 oz sun-dried tomatoes in oil, drained

50 g/1³/4 oz canned anchovy fillets, drained

pepper

55 g/2 oz sun-dried tomato paste

plain flour, for dusting

500 g/1 lb 2 oz ready-made puff pastry, thawed if frozen

beaten egg, to glaze

Preheat the oven to 200°C/400°F/Gas Mark 6. Cut the cheese into small dice measuring about 5 mm/¹/4 inch. Chop the olives, sun-dried tomatoes and anchovies into pieces about the same size as the cheese. Put all the chopped ingredients in a bowl, season with pepper to taste and gently mix together. Stir in the sun-dried tomato paste.

On a lightly floured work surface, thinly roll out the puff pastry. Using a plain, round 8-cm/3¹/4-inch cutter, cut into 18 rounds. Gently pile the trimmings together, roll out again, then cut out a further 8 rounds. Using a teaspoon, put a little of the prepared filling equally in the centre of each of the pastry rounds.

Dampen the edges of the pastry with a little water, then bring up the sides to cover the filling completely and pinch the edges together with your fingers to seal them. With the tip of a sharp knife, make a small slit in the top of each pastry. You can store the pastries in the refrigerator at this stage until you are ready to bake them.

Place the pastries on dampened baking trays and brush each with a little beaten egg to glaze. Bake in the oven for 10–15 minutes, or until golden brown, crisp and well risen. Serve the empanadillas piping hot, warm or cold.

fried manchego cheese

Manchego is Spain's most famous cheese. It is sold at various stages of its maturity,
although the most widely available is the firm, full-flavoured hard cheese,
as opposed to the soft, mild young cheese which is rarely found outside Spain.

SERVES 6–8 AS PART OF A TAPAS MEAL

200 g/7 oz Manchego cheese
3 tbsp plain flour
salt and pepper
1 egg
1 tsp water
85 g/3 oz fresh white or brown breadcrumbs
sunflower oil, for deep-frying

Slice the cheese into triangular shapes about 2 cm/3/4 inch thick or alternatively into cubes measuring about the same size. Put the flour in a polythene bag and season with salt and pepper to taste. Break the egg into a shallow dish and beat together with the water. Spread the breadcrumbs onto a plate.

Toss the cheese pieces in the flour so that they are evenly coated, then dip the cheese in the egg mixture. Finally, dip the cheese in the breadcrumbs so that the pieces are coated on all sides. Transfer to a large plate and store in the refrigerator until you are ready to serve them.

Just before serving, heat about 2.5 cm/1 inch of the sunflower oil in a large, heavy-based frying pan or heat the oil in a deep fryer to 180–190°C/350–375°F, or until a cube of bread browns in 30 seconds. Add the cheese, in batches of about 4 or 5 pieces so that the temperature of the oil does not drop, and fry for 1–2 minutes, turning once, until the cheese is just beginning to melt and the pieces are golden brown on all sides. Do make sure that the oil is hot enough, otherwise the coating on the cheese will take too long to become crisp and the cheese inside may ooze out.

Using a slotted spoon, remove the fried cheese from the frying pan or deep fryer and drain well on kitchen paper. Serve the fried cheese pieces hot, accompanied by cocktail sticks on which to spear them.

variation

Other cheeses work equally well here,
such as Cheddar, mozzarella or even
a firm goat's cheese.

devilled eggs

In the south of Spain, the selection of dishes served in tapas bars would be considered incomplete without the inclusion of these Devilled Eggs and Tortilla Española (see page 70). As a variation, you could use rolled, canned anchovy fillets to garnish each egg. *MAKES 16*

8 large eggs

2 whole pimientos

(sweet red peppers) from a jar or can

8 green olives

5 tbsp mayonnaise

8 drops Tabasco sauce

large pinch cayenne pepper

salt and pepper

paprika, for dusting

sprigs of fresh dill, to garnish

To cook the eggs, put them in a saucepan, cover with cold water and slowly bring to the boil. Immediately reduce the heat to very low, cover and simmer gently for 10 minutes. As soon as the eggs are cooked, drain them and put under cold running water until they are cold. By doing this quickly, it will prevent a black ring from forming around the egg yolk. Gently tap the eggs to crack the eggshells and leave them until cold. When cold, crack the shells all over and remove them.

Using a stainless steel knife, halve the eggs lengthways, then carefully remove the yolks. Put the yolks in a nylon sieve, set over a bowl, and rub through, then mash them with a wooden spoon or fork. If necessary, rinse the egg whites under cold water and dry very carefully.

Put the pimientos on kitchen paper to dry well, then chop them finely, reserving a few strips.

Finely chop the olives. If you are going to pipe the filling into the eggs, you need to chop both these ingredients very finely so that they will go through a 1-cm/$1^1/_2$-inch nozzle. Add the chopped pimientos and most of the chopped olives to the mashed egg yolks, reserving 16 larger pieces to garnish. Add the mayonnaise, mix well together, then add the Tabasco sauce, cayenne pepper and salt and pepper to taste.

Finally put the egg yolk mixture into a piping bag fitted with a 1-cm/$1/_2$-inch plain nozzle and pipe the mixture into the hollow egg whites. Alternatively, for a simpler finish, use a teaspoon to spoon the prepared filling into each egg half.

Arrange the eggs on a serving plate. Add a small strip of the reserved pimientos and a piece of olive to the top of each stuffed egg. Dust with a little paprika and garnish with dill sprigs.

tortilla española

This is Spain's classic tapa (as well as the staple food for a picnic) and is made with potato, onion and egg. Other ingredients can be added, such as ham, bacon, cheese, mushrooms, red or green peppers, asparagus and artichoke hearts, but the Spanish prefer to keep it plain. *SERVES 8 AS PART OF A TAPAS MEAL*

450 g/1 lb waxy potatoes
425 ml/15 fl oz Spanish olive oil
2 onions, chopped

2 large eggs
salt and pepper
sprigs of fresh flat-leaved parsley, to garnish

Peel the potatoes, cut into small cubes or wedges, then put on a clean tea towel and dry well. Heat the olive oil in a large, heavy-based or non-stick frying pan. Add the potato pieces and onions, then reduce the heat and fry the potatoes, stirring frequently so that they do not clump together, for 20 minutes, or until they are tender but not browned. The secret of success is to cook the potatoes for a long time so that they absorb the flavour of the oil and are cooked but not browned or crisp, and do not fall apart. They are, in fact, almost boiled rather than fried.

Meanwhile, beat the eggs lightly in a large bowl and season well with salt and pepper. Place a sieve over a large bowl.

When the potatoes and onions are cooked, drain them into the sieve so that the bowl catches the oil. Reserve the oil for future use. When the potatoes and onions are well drained, gently stir them into the beaten eggs.

Wipe the frying pan clean or wash it if necessary to prevent the tortilla from sticking. Heat 2 tablespoons of the reserved olive oil in the pan. When hot, add the egg and potato mixture, reduce the heat and cook for 3–5 minutes, or until the underside is just set. Use a spatula to push the potatoes down into the egg so that they are completely submerged, and keep loosening the tortilla from the base of the pan to stop it sticking.

To cook the second side of the tortilla, cover it with a plate and hold the plate in place with the other hand. Drain off the oil in the pan, then quickly turn the pan upside down so that the tortilla falls onto the plate. Return the frying pan to the heat and add a little more of the reserved oil to it if necessary. Slide the tortilla, cooked side uppermost, back into the pan and fry for a further 3–5 minutes, or until set underneath. The tortilla is cooked when it is firm and crisp on the outside but still slightly runny in the centre.

Slide the tortilla onto a serving plate and leave to stand for about 15 minutes. Serve it warm or cold, cut into small squares, fingers or wedges and garnished with parsley sprigs.

fish & seafood

HERE there are eleven recipes that draw on a wide selection of fish and seafood. Included are recipes using cod, salmon, sardines, monkfish, tuna, crab, prawns, calamares, scallops and mussels.

cod & caper croquettes

The secret of cooking croquettes successfully is to chill the mixture in the refrigerator before frying. You will then find that they do not disintegrate when put in the hot oil. As a matter of interest, Spain is the world's largest producer of capers! *MAKES 12*

350 g/12 oz white fish fillets, such as cod, haddock or monkfish

300 ml/10 fl oz milk

salt and pepper

4 tbsp olive oil or 55 g/2 oz butter

55 g/2 oz plain flour

4 tbsp capers, roughly chopped

1 tsp paprika

1 garlic clove, crushed

1 tsp lemon juice

3 tbsp chopped fresh flat-leaved parsley, plus extra sprigs to garnish

1 egg, beaten

55 g/2 oz fresh white breadcrumbs

1 tbsp sesame seeds

sunflower oil, for deep-frying

lemon wedges, to garnish

mayonnaise, to serve

Put the fish fillets in a large, heavy-based frying pan. Pour in the milk and season to taste with salt and pepper. Bring to the boil, then reduce the heat, cover the pan and simmer gently for 8–10 minutes, or until the fish flakes easily when tested with a fork. Using a fish slice, remove the fish fillets from the pan. Pour the milk into a jug and reserve for later. Flake the fish, removing and discarding the skin and bones.

Heat the olive oil in a saucepan. Stir in the flour to form a paste and cook gently, stirring, for 1 minute. Remove the saucepan from the heat and gradually stir in the reserved milk until smooth. Return to the heat and bring to the boil, stirring all the time, until the mixture thickens.

Remove the saucepan from the heat, add the flaked fish and beat until the mixture is smooth. Add the capers, paprika, garlic, lemon juice and parsley and mix well. Season the mixture to taste with salt and pepper. Spread the fish mixture in a dish and leave to cool, cover and put in the refrigerator for 2–3 hours or overnight.

When the fish mixture has chilled, pour the beaten egg onto a plate. Put the breadcrumbs and

sesame seeds on a separate plate, mix together and spread out. Divide the fish mixture into 12 equal-sized portions. With lightly floured hands, form each portion into a sausage shape, measuring about 7.5 cm/3 inches in length. Dip the croquettes, one at a time, in the beaten egg, roll in the breadcrumb mixture to coat them. Place on a plate and chill in the refrigerator for about 1 hour.

To cook the croquettes, heat the oil in a deep fryer to 180–190°C/350–375°F. Add the croquettes, in batches, and fry for 3 minutes. Remove from the pan with a slotted spoon and drain them well on kitchen paper.

Serve piping hot, garnished with lemon wedges and parsley sprigs and accompanied by a bowl of mayonnaise for dipping.

fresh salmon
in mojo sauce

Mojo sauce is also known as Canary Island Red Sauce, after its place of origin.
When served without the paprika but with finely chopped fresh coriander and parsley leaves,
it is known as Canary Island Green Sauce. It is also good drizzled over boiled new potatoes.

SERVES 8 AS PART OF A TAPAS MEAL

4 fresh salmon fillets, weighing
about 750 g/1 lb 10 oz in total
salt and pepper
3 tbsp Spanish olive oil
1 fresh flat-leaved parsley sprig, to garnish

Mojo Sauce
2 garlic cloves, peeled
2 tsp paprika
1 tsp ground cumin
5 tbsp Spanish extra virgin olive oil
2 tbsp white wine vinegar
salt

To prepare the mojo sauce, put the garlic, paprika and cumin in the bowl of a food processor fitted with the metal blade and, using a pulsing action, blend for 1 minute to mix well together. With the motor still running, add 1 tablespoon of the olive oil, drop by drop, through the feeder tube. When it

has been added, scrape down the sides of the bowl with a spatula, then very slowly continue to pour in the oil in a thin, steady stream, until all the oil has been added and the sauce has slightly thickened. Add the vinegar and blend for a further 1 minute. Season the sauce with salt to taste.

To prepare the salmon, remove the skin, cut each fillet in half widthways, then cut lengthways into 2-cm/3/4-inch thick slices, discarding any bones. Season the pieces of fish to taste with salt and pepper.

Heat the olive oil in a large, heavy-based frying pan. When hot, add the pieces of fish and fry for about 10 minutes, depending on its thickness, turning occasionally until cooked and browned on both sides.

Transfer the salmon to a warmed serving dish, drizzle over some of the mojo sauce and serve hot, garnished with parsley and accompanied by the remaining sauce in a small serving bowl.

sardines marinated in sherry vinegar

Sherry vinegar is ideal for marinating fish such as sardines, trout or salmon.

SERVES 6 AS PART OF A TAPAS MEAL

12 small fresh sardines

175 ml/6 fl oz Spanish olive oil

4 tbsp sherry vinegar

2 carrots, cut into julienne strips

1 onion, thinly sliced

1 garlic clove, crushed

1 bay leaf

salt and pepper

4 tbsp chopped fresh flat-leaved parsley

few sprigs of fresh dill, to garnish

lemon wedges, to serve

If it has not already been done, clean the fish by scraping the scales off with a knife, being careful not to cut the skin. The choice is yours whether you then leave the heads and tails on or cut them off and discard. Slit along the belly of each fish and remove the innards under cold running water. Then dry each fish well on kitchen paper.

Heat 4 tablespoons of the olive oil in a large, heavy-based frying pan. Add the sardines and fry for 10 minutes, or until browned on both sides. Using a fish slice, very carefully remove the sardines from the pan and transfer to a large, shallow, non-metallic dish that will hold the sardines in a single layer.

Gently heat the remaining olive oil and the sherry vinegar in a large saucepan, add the carrot strips, onion, garlic and bay leaf and simmer gently for 5 minutes, or until softened. Season the vegetables to taste with salt and pepper. Allow the mixture to cool slightly, then pour the marinade over the sardines.

Cover the dish and let the sardines cool before transferring to the refrigerator. Leave to marinate for about 8 hours or overnight, spooning the marinade over the sardines occasionally, although there is no need to get up in the night! Return the sardines to room temperature before serving, sprinkle with parsley and garnish with dill sprigs. Serve with lemon wedges.

variation

Fresh trout or salmon fillets can be used, but instead of frying the fish, it is better to steam the fillets for 5 minutes. When cooked, slice each fillet in half lengthways. You will need 6 fish fillets in total for this recipe.

monkfish, rosemary & bacon skewers

Monkfish is ideal for skewers because of its firm texture, but other firm-fleshed fish, such as cod, swordfish or tuna, would make ideal alternatives. Instead of using rosemary stalks, you can use the more traditional metal skewers or wooden bamboo skewers. The latter should be pre-soaked in cold water for 30 minutes to prevent them from burning. *MAKES 12*

350 g/12 oz monkfish tail or 250 g/9 oz monkfish fillet

12 stalks of fresh rosemary

3 tbsp Spanish olive oil

juice of ½ small lemon

1 garlic clove, crushed

salt and pepper

6 thick back bacon rashers

lemon wedges, to garnish

Aïoli (see page 53), to serve

If using monkfish tail, cut either side of the central bone with a sharp knife and remove the flesh to form 2 fillets. Slice the fillets in half lengthways, then cut each fillet into 12 bite-sized chunks to give a total of 24 pieces. Put the monkfish pieces in a large bowl.

To prepare the rosemary skewers, strip the leaves off the stalks and reserve them, leaving a few leaves at one end.

For the marinade, finely chop the reserved leaves and whisk together in a bowl with the olive oil, lemon juice, garlic and salt and pepper to taste. Add the monkfish pieces and toss until coated in the marinade. Cover and leave to marinate in the refrigerator for 1–2 hours.

Cut each bacon rasher in half lengthways, then in half widthways, and roll up each piece. Thread 2 pieces of monkfish alternately with 2 bacon rolls onto the prepared rosemary skewers.

Preheat the grill, griddle or barbecue. If you are cooking the skewers under an overhead grill, arrange them on the grill pan so that the leaves of the rosemary skewers protrude from the grill and therefore do not catch fire during cooking. Grill the monkfish and bacon skewers for 10 minutes, turning from time to time and basting with any remaining marinade, or until cooked. Serve hot, garnished with lemon wedges for squeezing over them and accompanied by a bowl of Aïoli in which to dip the monkfish skewers.

tuna with
pimiento-stuffed olives

Now that tuna can easily be bought fresh, it is a real treat. It has a firm flesh and a superb flavour. Once cooked – grilled, fried, baked or braised – you can eat it as a steak or exactly the same way as you would canned tuna. *SERVES 6 AS PART OF A TAPAS MEAL*

2 fresh tuna steaks, weighing about 250 g/
9 oz in total and about 2.5 cm/1 inch thick

5 tbsp Spanish olive oil

3 tbsp red wine vinegar

4 sprigs of fresh thyme, plus extra to garnish

1 bay leaf

salt and pepper

2 tbsp plain flour

1 onion, finely chopped

2 garlic cloves, finely chopped

85 g/3 oz pimiento-stuffed green olives, sliced

crusty bread, to serve

Do not get caught out with this recipe – the tuna steaks need to be marinated, so remember to start preparing the dish the day before you are going to serve it. Remove the skin from the tuna steaks, then cut the steaks in half along the grain of the fish. Cut each half into 1-cm/$^1/_2$-inch thick slices against the grain.

Put 3 tablespoons of the olive oil and the vinegar in a large, shallow, non-metallic dish.

Strip the leaves from the sprigs of thyme and add these to the dish with the bay leaf and salt and pepper to taste. Add the prepared strips of tuna, cover the dish and leave to marinate in the refrigerator for 8 hours or overnight.

The next day, put the flour in a polythene bag. Remove the tuna strips from the marinade, reserving the marinade for later, add them to the bag of flour and toss well until they are lightly coated.

Heat the remaining olive oil in a large, heavy-based frying pan. Add the onion and garlic and gently fry for 5–10 minutes, or until softened and golden brown. Add the tuna strips to the pan and fry for 2–5 minutes, turning several times, until the fish becomes opaque. Add the reserved marinade and olives to the pan and cook for a further 1–2 minutes, stirring, until the fish is tender and the sauce has thickened.

Serve the tuna and olives piping hot, garnished with thyme sprigs. Accompany with slices of crusty bread for mopping up the sauce.

crab tartlets

You only have to look along the shelves of a Spanish supermarket to see the numerous varieties of canned fish that are available. On that note, canned salmon or tuna could easily be used in this recipe in place of the crabmeat. *MAKES 24*

1 tbsp Spanish olive oil

1 small onion, finely chopped

1 garlic clove, finely chopped

splash of dry white wine

2 eggs

150 ml/5 fl oz milk or single cream

175 g/6 oz canned crabmeat, drained

55 g/2 oz Manchego or Parmesan cheese, grated

2 tbsp chopped fresh flat-leaved parsley

pinch of freshly grated nutmeg

salt and pepper

sprigs of fresh dill, to garnish

Pastry

350 g/12 oz plain flour, plus extra for dusting

pinch of salt

175 g/6 oz butter

2 tbsp cold water

OR

500 g/1 lb 2 oz ready-made shortcrust pastry

Preheat the oven to 190°C/375°F/Gas Mark 5. To prepare the crabmeat filling, heat the olive oil in a saucepan, add the onion and fry for 5 minutes, or until softened but not browned. Add the garlic and fry for a further 30 seconds. Add a splash of wine and cook for 1–2 minutes, or until most of the wine has evaporated.

Lightly whisk the eggs in a large mixing bowl, then whisk in the milk or cream. Add the crabmeat, cheese, parsley and the onion mixture. Season the mixture with nutmeg and salt and pepper to taste and mix well together.

To prepare the pastry if you are making it yourself, mix the flour and salt together in a large mixing bowl. Add the butter, cut into small pieces, and rub in until the mixture resembles fine breadcrumbs. Gradually stir in enough of the water to form a firm dough. Alternatively, the pastry could be made in a food processor.

On a lightly floured work surface, thinly roll out the pastry. Using a plain, round 7-cm/2³/4-inch cutter, cut the pastry into 18 rounds. Gently pile the trimmings together, roll out again, then cut out a further 6 rounds. Use to line 24 x 4-cm/ 1¹/2-inch tartlet tins.

Carefully spoon the crabmeat mixture into the pastry cases, taking care not to overfill them.

Bake the tartlets in the oven for 25–30 minutes until browned and set. Then serve the crab tartlets hot or cold, garnished with fresh dill sprigs.

lime-drizzled prawns

This dish can also be prepared with cooked fresh or frozen prawns. Make sure that you dry them very well on kitchen paper before using and, as they are already cooked, add them to the pan for just 1–2 minutes, simply to heat them through.

SERVES 6 AS PART OF A TAPAS MEAL

4 limes

12 raw tiger prawns, in their shells

3 tbsp Spanish olive oil

2 garlic cloves, finely chopped

splash of dry sherry

salt and pepper

4 tbsp chopped fresh flat-leaved parsley

Grate the rind and squeeze out the juice from 2 of the limes. Cut the remaining 2 limes into wedges and reserve for later.

To prepare the prawns, remove the legs, leaving the shells and tails intact. Using a sharp knife, make a shallow slit along the top of each

prawn, then pull out the dark vein and discard. Rinse the prawns under cold water and dry well on kitchen paper.

Heat the olive oil in a large, heavy-based frying pan, then add the garlic and fry for 30 seconds. Add the prawns and fry for 5 minutes, stirring from time to time, or until they turn pink and begin to curl. Mix in the lime rind, juice and a splash of sherry to moisten, then stir well.

Transfer the cooked prawns to a serving dish, season to taste with salt and pepper and sprinkle over the parsley. Serve piping hot, accompanied by the reserved lime wedges for squeezing over the prawns.

sizzling chilli prawns

The point of this dish is that the pan is brought to the table and the prawns are served really hot, hence their name. The oil should still be sizzling, and so it is usually served with a plate of bread perched on top.

SERVES 8 AS PART OF A TAPAS MEAL

To prepare the prawns, pull off their heads. With your fingers, peel off their shells, leaving the tails intact. Using a sharp knife, make a shallow slit along the top of each prawn, then pull out the dark vein and discard. Rinse the prawns under cold water and dry well on kitchen paper.

Cut the chilli in half lengthways, remove the seeds and finely chop the flesh. It is important either to wear gloves or to wash your hands very thoroughly after chopping chillies, as their juices can cause irritation to sensitive skin, especially around the eyes, nose or mouth. Whatever you do, do not rub your eyes after touching the cut flesh of the chilli.

Heat the olive oil in a large, heavy-based frying pan or flameproof casserole until quite hot, then add the garlic and fry for 30 seconds. Add the prawns, chilli, paprika and a pinch of salt and fry for 2–3 minutes, stirring all the time, until the prawns turn pink and begin to curl.

Serve the prawns in the cooking dish, still sizzling. Accompany with cocktail sticks, to spear the prawns, and chunks or slices of crusty bread to mop up the aromatic cooking oil.

500 g/1 lb 2 oz raw tiger prawns, in their shells
1 small fresh red chilli
6 tbsp Spanish olive oil
2 garlic cloves, finely chopped
pinch of paprika
salt
crusty bread, to serve

calamares

Squid is available already prepared and sliced into rings, but if you have the time it is better to prepare it yourself. *SERVES 6 AS PART OF A TAPAS MEAL*

450 g/1 lb prepared squid (see cook's tip)

plain flour, for coating

sunflower oil, for deep-frying

salt

lemon wedges, to garnish

Aïoli (see page 53), to serve

Slice the squid into 1-cm/¹/₂-inch rings and halve the tentacles if large. Rinse and dry well on kitchen paper so that they do not spit during cooking. Dust the squid pieces with flour so that they are lightly coated. Do not season the flour, as Spanish cooks will tell you that seasoning squid with salt before cooking toughens it. They should know!

Heat the sunflower oil in a deep fryer to 180–190°C/350–375°F, or until a cube of bread

browns in 30 seconds. Carefully add the squid pieces, in batches so that the temperature of the oil does not drop, and fry for 2–3 minutes, or until golden brown and crisp all over, turning several times. Do not overcook, or the squid will become tough and rubbery rather than moist and tender.

Using a slotted spoon, remove the fried squid from the deep fryer and drain well on kitchen paper. Keep warm in the oven while you fry the remaining squid pieces.

Sprinkle the fried squid pieces with salt and serve piping hot, garnished with lemon wedges for squeezing over them. Accompany with a bowl of Aïoli in which to dip the calamares.

cook's tip

If you need to prepare the squid yourself, hold the body in one hand and pull on the head and tentacles with the other. The body contents will come away too and can be discarded. Cut off the edible tentacles just above the eyes and discard the head. Remove the ink sacs from the head carefully so that you do not pierce them. Remove the backbone and peel off the thin, dark outer skin.

scallops in saffron sauce

Shelled scallops are available, both fresh and frozen, from supermarkets and fishmongers. Should you buy them from a fishmonger, ask if you can have some shells, as they make attractive serving dishes. You will need to scrub them clean before use.

SERVES 8 AS PART OF A TAPAS MEAL

150 ml/5 fl oz dry white wine

150 ml/5 fl oz fish stock

large pinch of saffron strands

900 g/2 lb shelled scallops, preferably large ones

salt and pepper

3 tbsp Spanish olive oil

1 small onion, finely chopped

2 garlic cloves, finely chopped

150 ml/5 fl oz double cream

squeeze of lemon juice

chopped fresh flat-leaved parsley, to garnish

crusty bread, to serve

Put the wine, fish stock and saffron in a saucepan and bring to the boil. Reduce the heat, cover and simmer gently for 15 minutes.

Meanwhile, remove and discard from each scallop the tough, white muscle that is found opposite the coral, and separate the coral from the scallop. Slice the scallops vertically into thick slices, including the corals if they are present. Dry the scallops well on kitchen paper, then season to taste with salt and pepper.

Heat the olive oil in a large, heavy-based frying pan. Add the onion and garlic and fry for 5 minutes, or until softened and lightly browned. Add the sliced scallops to the pan and fry gently for 5 minutes, stirring occasionally, or until they just turn opaque. The secret is not to overcook the scallops; otherwise they will become tough and rubbery.

Using a slotted spoon, remove the scallops from the pan and transfer to a warmed plate. Add the saffron liquid to the pan, bring to the boil and boil rapidly until reduced to about half. Reduce the heat and gradually stir in the cream, just a little at a time. Simmer gently until the sauce thickens.

Return the scallops to the pan and simmer for 1–2 minutes just to heat them through. Add a squeeze of lemon juice and season to taste with salt and pepper. Serve the scallops hot, garnished with the parsley and accompanied by chunks or slices of crusty bread to mop up the saffron sauce.

mussels with
herb & garlic butter

Due to the lack of lush pastureland in most of Spain, dairy cattle are not
extensively raised and therefore oil, as opposed to butter, is more commonly used in cooking.
Nevertheless, butter is occasionally used, as illustrated in this recipe.

SERVES 8 AS PART OF A TAPAS MEAL

800 g/1 lb 12 oz fresh mussels, in their shells

splash of dry white wine

1 bay leaf

85 g/3 oz butter

35 g/1^1/$_4$ oz fresh white or brown breadcrumbs

4 tbsp chopped fresh flat-leaved parsley,
plus extra sprigs to garnish

2 tbsp snipped fresh chives

2 garlic cloves, finely chopped

salt and pepper

lemon wedges, to serve

Clean the mussels by scrubbing or scraping the shells and pulling out any beards that are attached to them. Discard any with broken shells and any that refuse to close when tapped. Put the mussels in a colander and rinse well under cold running water. Preheat the oven to 230°C/450°F/Gas Mark 8.

Put the mussels in a large saucepan and add a splash of wine and the bay leaf. Cook, covered, over a high heat for 5 minutes, shaking the saucepan occasionally, or until the mussels are opened. Drain the mussels and discard any that remain closed.

Shell the mussels, reserving one half of each shell. Arrange the mussels, in their half-shells, in a large, shallow, ovenproof serving dish.

Melt the butter and pour into a small bowl. Add the breadcrumbs, parsley, chives, garlic and salt and pepper to taste and mix well together. Leave until the butter has set slightly. Using your fingers or 2 teaspoons, take a large pinch of the herb and butter mixture and use to fill each

mussel shell, pressing it down well. Chill the filled mussels in the refrigerator until ready to serve.

To serve, bake the mussels in the oven for 10 minutes, or until hot. Serve immediately, garnished with parsley sprigs and accompanied by lemon wedges for squeezing over them.

index